{IT CHANGED THE WORLD}

INVENTION OF
FLIGHT

Mike Downs

Rourke
Educational Media

A Division of
Carson Dellosa
Education

rourkeeducationalmedia.com

ROURKE'S
SCHOOL to HOME
CONNECTIONS
BEFORE AND DURING READING ACTIVITIES

Before Reading: *Building Background Knowledge and Vocabulary*

Building background knowledge can help children process new information and build upon what they already know. Before reading a book, it is important to tap into what children already know about the topic. This will help them develop their vocabulary and increase their reading comprehension.

Questions and Activities to Build Background Knowledge:

1. Look at the front cover of the book and read the title. What do you think this book will be about?
2. What do you already know about this topic?
3. Take a book walk and skim the pages. Look at the table of contents, photographs, captions, and bold words. Did these text features give you any information or predictions about what you will read in this book?

Vocabulary: *Vocabulary Is Key to Reading Comprehension*

Use the following directions to prompt a conversation about each word.

- Read the vocabulary words.
- What comes to mind when you see each word?
- What do you think each word means?

> ### Vocabulary Words:
> - aircraft
> - aircraft carriers
> - airmail
> - aviation
> - contrails
> - hang gliders
> - jet engines
> - pesticides
> - reconnaissance
> - simulators

During Reading: *Reading for Meaning and Understanding*

To achieve deep comprehension of a book, children are encouraged to use close reading strategies. During reading, it is important to have children stop and make connections. These connections result in deeper analysis and understanding of a book.

Close Reading a Text

During reading, have children stop and talk about the following:

- Any confusing parts
- Any unknown words
- Text to text, text to self, text to world connections
- The main idea in each chapter or heading

Encourage children to use context clues to determine the meaning of any unknown words. These strategies will help children learn to analyze the text more thoroughly as they read.

When you are finished reading this book, turn to the next-to-last page for **Text-Dependent Questions** and an **Extension Activity**.

TABLE OF CONTENTS

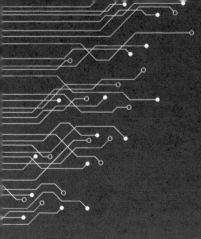

ARE WE THERE YET?

Look at the sky. On a clear day, you might see crisscrossing white lines, or **contrails**. Contrails are made by airplane engines, but they aren't smoke. Contrails are tiny particles of ice.

The first contrails were seen about 110 years ago. That's because powered airplanes didn't exist until then. Imagine traveling long distances without an airplane. Traveling hundreds or thousands of miles on a horse or wagon could take weeks or months. How many times would you ask, "Are we there yet?"

Before the powered airplane was invented, many people walked. Others rode bicycles, horses, or carriages because only a few people had cars. For long-distance trips, people rode trains, and steam-powered ships crossed the oceans. At this point, flying was only a dream.

FLY LIKE A BIRD

Some people thought that the key to flight was flapping wings, like birds do. But birds weigh less than humans and have wings that work in a special way. People would need huge wings to lift their weight, and the giant wings would be too heavy to use.

Many early inventors tried to fly by using flapping motions. Some strapped wings to their arms, while others made unusual machines that flapped. These methods didn't work.

Otto Lilienthal was a German inventor who created flying machines. Some of these had wings that flapped. He tested them on a hill he built near his home.

THE FIRST AIR MACHINES

The first successful flights happened when people flew by hanging under huge kites. These flights were followed by the flights of hot air balloons and **hang gliders**. But none of these could be steered exactly where the pilots wanted to go. They were all affected by the direction the wind was blowing.

Many inventors tried to build airplanes powered by
engines. The idea of a powered plane is that they can move
forward quickly enough that the air on the top of the wing
pushes it down, and the air underneath the wing pushes up.

Orville Wright

This difference creates lift, which brings the plane into the air. In 1903, Orville and Wilbur Wright were the first to successfully build and fly a powered plane.

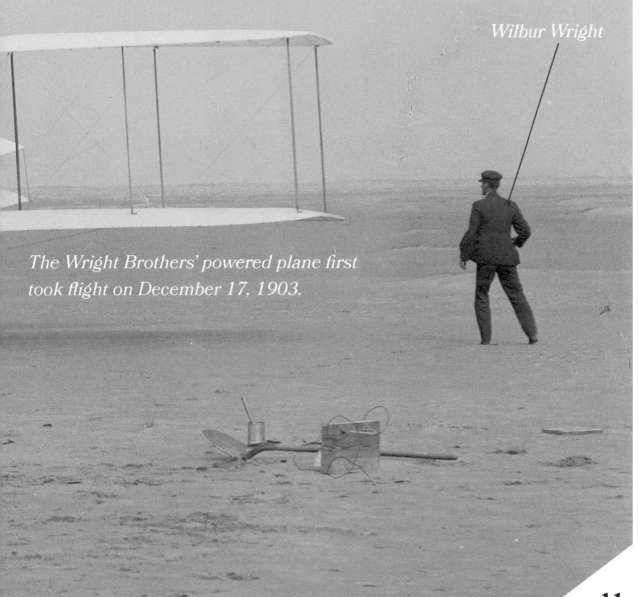

Wilbur Wright

The Wright Brothers' powered plane first took flight on December 17, 1903.

At first, many people didn't believe that the Wright brothers had flown. Some thought building a powered airplane was impossible. Others thought the Wright brothers were lying. Years after their first flight, the news began to spread, and then everybody was amazed.

In less than 15 years, airplanes were everywhere. The first official **airmail** flight was used in India in 1911. The first scheduled airline flight for passengers, on which a single passenger flew, occurred in the United States in 1914.

Airplanes changed how wars were fought and played an important role in World War I (WWI). They were used for **reconnaissance** to see what the enemy was doing. They were also used as bombers and fighters.

BRAVERY IN THE SKY

Bessie Coleman was a famous African American and Native American stunt pilot in the 1920s. In 1921, she became the first woman of either of these backgrounds to hold a pilot's license. She had an incredible career flying in air shows and was known as someone who would stop at nothing to perform a stunt. She worked for equality in flight and education until her death in a plane crash in 1926.

After WWI, planes were used in the circus. These circuses were different from the ones you're probably thinking of. Pilots put on airshows and gave airplane rides. Sometimes, entire towns closed for the day so everyone could watch. Many townspeople had never seen airplanes before.

But early planes weren't only used to entertain. Farmers found an important use for them when pilots put **pesticides** in their planes and flew over fields. They dusted the crops to kill insects, which earned the machines the name *crop dusters*.

BIGGER, BETTER, FASTER

Governments started using more military planes, but most planes couldn't fly very far. To overcome this problem, ships that could carry **aircraft** were invented. With **aircraft carriers**, a government could send airplanes around the world. The first aircraft carrier was built in Japan in 1922.

Airplanes played a huge role in World War II (WWII). Japan used them to attack Pearl Harbor. Germany and the Allies fought each other with bomber planes and fighter planes.

After WWII, planes got bigger and faster. Airplanes with **jet engines** were invented and improved, as were airliners that could hold hundreds of people. Countries built large airports because they wanted airplanes to bring travelers who would spend money in their countries. The use of airplanes encouraged business around the world.

MASSIVE AIRLINERS

Many large jets can carry more than 300 passengers. The Airbus A380 can normally carry about 550 passengers. It can be outfitted to carry over 850 people. That's enough to make up a small town!

AVIATION EVERYWHERE

Jet airliners allowed people to fly to places they had only dreamed about. Jet engines make planes fly by using burning fuel to spin a wheel at high speeds, pushing the plane forward. Planes with these engines could get anywhere in the world in less than two days. People could see volcanoes in Hawaii, go on safari in Africa, and visit castles in Europe or temples in Japan.

Packages traveled faster by air too. Instead of taking weeks, packages arrived in days. Then, package delivery companies developed systems to deliver packages overnight.

Concorde planes fly faster than the speed of sound.

Soon after, helicopters were part of the **aviation** revolution. Helicopter cranes lifted massive loads for construction projects. Police helicopters were used to chase suspects. Rescue helicopters were used to save people from sinking ships, mountaintops, and floods.

Aircraft were used to help fight wildfires as pilots learned to fly overhead and dump fire retardant. Pilots also flew aircraft carrying firefighters. The firefighters, called *smoke jumpers*, could parachute down to land near the fire.

A helicopter drops water onto a forest. A heavy load, right, is lifted with a helicopter.

The growth of aviation introduced amazing new careers. Pilots, airplane mechanics, parachute jumpers, air traffic controllers, flight attendants, and astronauts are just a few. What aviation job would you like to have?

THE FUTURE

Airplanes are changing every day and involve more computers and other technology. New aircraft have glass cockpits. This allows multiple liquid crystal display (LCD) screens to give pilots vital information.

As new planes get bigger and more expensive to fly, training also gets more expensive. Airlines use **simulators** to save money. Airline simulators have controls exactly like the real airplane. After simulator training, a pilot can safely fly the real plane on the first try.

Helicopter simulators can be used for pilot training.

SIMULATOR SUCCESS

Using simulators helps pilots learn faster and become better at flying planes. With special computers, pilots can practice turning and landing, taking off, and even rescuing a plane when there is unexpected danger. All of this is done without putting anyone at risk. Some people even use simulators to learn about flying in their own home!

Lots of people pilot small aircraft. Some fly small powered planes, while others fly sailplanes, hang gliders, or powered parachutes. Daring flyers jump out of planes wearing wingsuits that let them soar like flying squirrels.

THE HUMAN JET

Yves Rossy straps on wings and jet engines. He flies like a plane. He has even flown in formation with the huge Airbus A380 airliner.

Aircraft also fly without pilots. These aircraft, called *drones*, are taking over many flying jobs. Some drones can be flown from thousands of miles away. They can be used for spying, monitoring weather, or shooting weapons. Many are used for taking pictures or videos.

Aviation has given us better travel, technology, and entertainment. But there is no doubt that new advancements in flight will continue to change the world. Incredible inventions will be created by our next generation—maybe including you!

GLOSSARY

aircraft (AIR-kraft): airplanes, helicopters, gliders, or other machines capable of flight

aircraft carriers (AIR-kraft KAR-ee-urz): ships with large decks that are used for aircraft to land and take off

airmail (AIR-mayl): the service that delivers letters and packages carried by aircraft

aviation (ay-vee-AY-shuhn): the practice and science of building and flying aircraft

contrails (KAHN-trayls): streaks of ice particles created by water vapor in jet engine exhaust gases

hang gliders (hang GLYE-durz): flying machines that work like a large kite and allow a person to fly by hanging underneath

jet engines (jet ehn-JINZ): engines powered by streams of gases made by burning fuel and air inside the engine

pesticides (PES-ti-sides): poisons used to kill insects

reconnaissance (ri-KAH-nuh-zuhns): watching enemies to see what they are doing

simulators (SIM-yuh-lay-turs): machines or computer programs used for training people in normal and emergency procedures

INDEX

TEXT-DEPENDENT QUESTIONS

1. How did jet airliners change people's lives?
2. Why are aircraft so important to the military?
3. What were some of the earliest flying machines?
4. How is technology important to flight today?
5. Why did early "flapping" methods of human flight fail?

EXTENSION ACTIVITY

Make a list of activities and careers related to aviation. Rank them from least to most dangerous. Decide which of the items you would like to do. Why do those activities and careers interest you most?

ABOUT THE AUTHOR

Mike Downs loves to fly! He has flown fighters, airliners, hang gliders, and tow-planes. Wingsuits are next on his list. He also loves to write for children. When he's not off on an adventure, he's busy writing books.

www.rourkeeducationalmedia.com

PHOTO CREDIT: Cover: ©Nastco, © Senior Airman Gracie Lee; pages 4-5: ©Ramiro Marquez Photos; page 6a: ©Vladis Chern; page 6b: ©Kenneth Canning; page 7: ©KellyNelson; page 8: ©Wiki; page 9: ©hyside; page 10-11, 12-13: ©LOC; page 12: ©peterspiro; page 14: ©Keith Tarrier; page 14b: ©Everett Collection/Newscom; page 15: ©Andy_Oxley; page 16: ©Shtrunts; page 17: ©CrackerClips; page 18: ©Everett Historical; page 19: ©Cylonphoto; page 20: ©jpgfactory; page 20a: ©np_limit_photos; page 21: ©Stockcam; page 22: ©Shaunl; page 23: ©Kemter; page 24: ©NASA; page 25: ©Kiwis; page 26: ©Sushitskey Sergey; page 27: ©SindreEspejord; page 27b: ©ueuaphoto; page 28: ©SipaUSA/Newscom

Edited by: Tracie Santos
Cover and interior layout by: Kathy Walsh

Library of Congress PCN Data

Invention of Flight / Mike Downs
(It Changed the World)
ISBN 978-1-73162-979-1 (hard cover)(alk. paper)
ISBN 978-1-73162-973-9 (soft cover)
ISBN 978-1-73162-985-2 (e-Book)
ISBN 978-1-73163-332-3 (ePub)
Library of Congress Control Number: 2019945507

Rourke Educational Media
Printed in the USA
02-0272313053